Vanilla Extract
flour
Vinegar
Salt
Baking Soda
Vegetable oil
Sugar
Cocoa Powder

Vanilla Extract
flour
Vinegar
Salt
Baking Soda
Vegetable Oil
Sugar
Cocoa Powder

# Meet Lottie

Lottie is a kind-hearted and polite little girl.
She is caring and considerate towards all animals and people but especially has a soft spot for babies and the elderly. She loves horses, drawing, playing with her older brother Brodie, and most of all, baking in the kitchen with Mommy.

For Ryan, who gives me strength,
for Charlotte, who brings me joy,
for Rowan, who gives me courage.

-R.B.

Text copyright © 2022 Rose Bakewell
Illustrations copyright © 2022 Joannie Studio

All rights reserved. No part of this book may be used or reproduced in any manner whatsoever without written permission except in the case of brief quotations embodied in critical articles and reviews.

Hardcover: 978-1-7366557-2-6

Author and Creative director: Rose Bakewell
Illustrator: Joannie Laroche
Copy editor: Mark Farrell

Publisher: Country Cottage Books

Country
Cottage
Books

# Lottie
## and the Baby

By
Rose Bakewell

Illustrated by
Joannie Laroche

"Is it time?"
Lottie and Brodie paced around the house, glancing up at every clock as they walked by each room.

"Is it time yet?" Lottie asked again, panicked.

"For the hundredth time, no," Granny Beth said, smiling.
"Come on over, you two, and have some milk and cookies."

Brodie sat down at the table and reached for a gingerbread cookie shaped like a baby rattle.

Lottie was too nervous to eat anything; not even Granny's famous gingerbread. All she could think about was that she was going to be a big sister.

"Mmm, these are really good," Brodie said, grabbing another cookie. "You should try one, Lotts."

"Why are they taking so long?" Lottie asked. "Mommy and Daddy should be home with the baby by now. Do you think they're okay? What if something's wrong?"

Granny could see that Lottie was getting a bit frantic. "Now, now, everything will be just fine," she said, comforting her.

Lottie continued pacing around the kitchen.

"I think this would be a perfect time to go water the garden," Granny said cheerfully. "Any volunteers?

"Me!" Brodie said, wiping the crumbs off of his mouth.

"Thank you for the cookies, Granny. They were delicious."

"You're so welcome, dear. I'm glad you enjoyed them," she said.

"How about you, Lottie? Would you like to help?"

Lottie didn't want to water the garden, nor did she want a cookie. Mommy and Daddy had left for the hospital the day before, and all she wanted was for them to be home with the baby, but she went along with Brodie and Granny anyway.

Brodie took the watering can and filled it with water. "Brodie, will you water the herbs, please, while Lottie and I harvest some vegetables?" Granny asked, picking up a willow basket and a trowel.

"Sure thing, Granny," Brodie said, walking over to the herb garden.

"Take a look at this, Lottie," Granny said, pointing to the beets. "Do you see how the roots are peeping up above the ground? That's how we know they're ready to be picked."

"Ooh, that's interesting," Lottie said, taking a closer look.

Granny slid the trowel into the dirt, gently tugged on the green leaves, and pulled out a lovely red beet.

Soon, the willow basket was full of beets, carrots, and zucchini.

"Do you think Mommy and Daddy are on their way home with the baby now?" Lottie asked.
"Should we call them again?" Brodie asked while rinsing the dirt off of the vegetables.

Granny had hoped to keep the children busy in the garden so they wouldn't spend so much time and energy worrying about things they had no control over.

"I'm sure they'll be home very soon," she said while trying to think of another way to help pass the time. "What do you say we make something yummy with these vegetables?"

"How about a vegetable stir fry?" Brodie suggested.
"Or maybe chocolate beetroot cake!" said Lottie.
"Even better!" Brodie said.

"Granny, remember when Lottie and I were allergic to eggs and dairy?" he asked. "Mommy would make us a vegan chocolate cake with beets in them!"

"I sure do remember those days," Granny said. "It was a terrifying time for your mother, and she was so determined to come up with a healthy cake recipe safe for you and Lottie to eat on your birthdays."

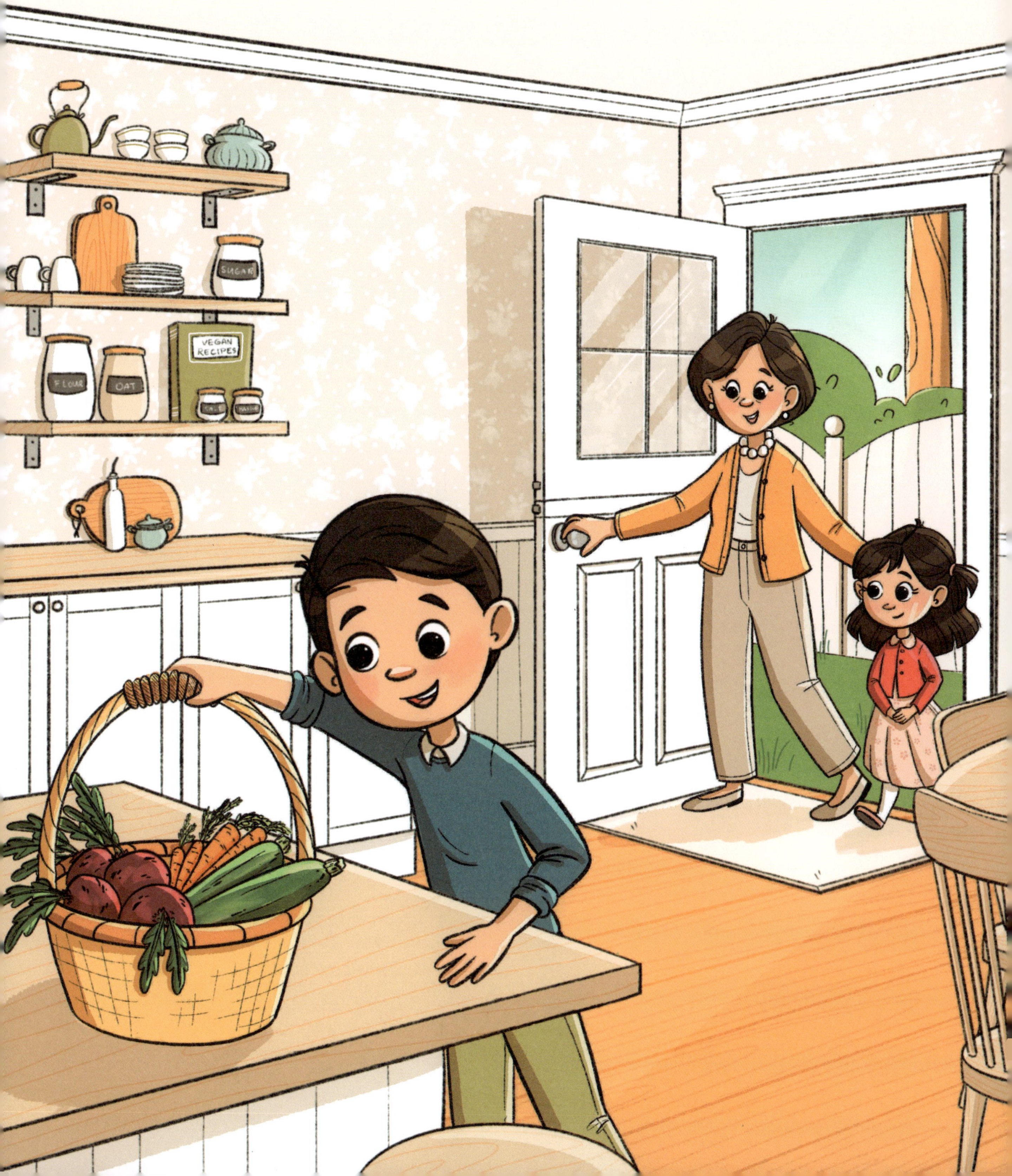
SUGAR
VEGAN RECIPES
FLOUR
OAT

Lottie opened Mommy's recipe box and found the chocolate beetroot cake recipe.

Brodie turned the oven on and gathered the ingredients while Granny peeled the beets.

Lottie sifted some **flour**, **sugar**, **cocoa powder**, **baking soda**, and **salt** together.

"I'll get the wet ingredients ready," Brodie said as he combined the **water**, **vegetable oil**, **vinegar**, and **vanilla extract** in a large measuring cup.

Meanwhile, Granny grated the **beets** and placed them into a bowl.

"Now, all we have to do is combine everything," said Lottie. Brodie poured the wet ingredients into the dry ingredients as Lottie mixed the batter with a whisk.

"Granny, would you like to stir in the beets?" Brodie asked, handing her a spatula.

"Why, it would be my pleasure, sire," she said in a regal tone, bowing playfully to get a laugh out of the children.

While the cake was baking in the oven, Granny explained the science behind how this cake could rise even without the use of eggs.

"The baking soda and vinegar react together and create tiny bubbles," she said.

She let Lottie and Brodie put a spoonful of baking soda and some vinegar into a bowl to experiment.

"It bubbles up like a volcano!" Lottie exclaimed.
"Wow!" said Brodie. "I'm going to use this trick for my next science project!"

"BEEP! BEEP!" The oven timer went off.

Granny removed the cake from the oven and set it on a cooling rack.

While the cake was cooling, Brodie and Lottie made the chocolate ganache by melting some **dark chocolate** and **oat milk** together and carefully poured it over the cake.

"May I please write something on the cake?" asked Lottie. "Of course!" Granny said. "I'll melt some white chocolate so you can pipe it on."

Lottie took her time writing a message on the cake and decided it needed something more.

She was scattering heart-shaped sprinkles around the edge when she heard a familiar voice.

"Look who's home," Daddy sang softly, holding a car seat in his hands.

Mommy slowly walked into the kitchen with the baby bundled up in her arms.

"Mommy!" Lottie and Brodie ran over and gave Mommy the biggest hug they had ever given her. "We missed you so much!"

"I missed you both too," Mommy said, smiling, and sat down so the children could say hello to their new baby brother.

"Aww, he is so cute!" they both said at the same time.

"Something smells delicious," Daddy said, looking over at the counter.

"We made a cake for the baby!" said Lottie.

"Granny also taught us that worrying doesn't help pass the time," said Brodie.

"It is important to sit with your emotions and allow yourself to feel them, but sometimes it's helpful to just be productive," Granny said.

"Now, let me see my gorgeous grandson," she said, overjoyed, and swept the baby from Mommy.

After dinner, Lottie got a chance to hold the baby while Granny and Daddy tidied the kitchen.

She looked into his beautiful brown eyes and couldn't believe how adorable he was. He had a cute little button nose, the sweetest little chin, and big round cheeks which she thought looked like fluffy marshmallows.

Mommy brought the cake over and placed it down on the table for dessert.

"I know you're too little to eat this right now," Lottie whispered. "But, when you get a little older, just ask your big sister, and I'll bake you anything you want."

She kissed the baby's forehead and showed him the cake.

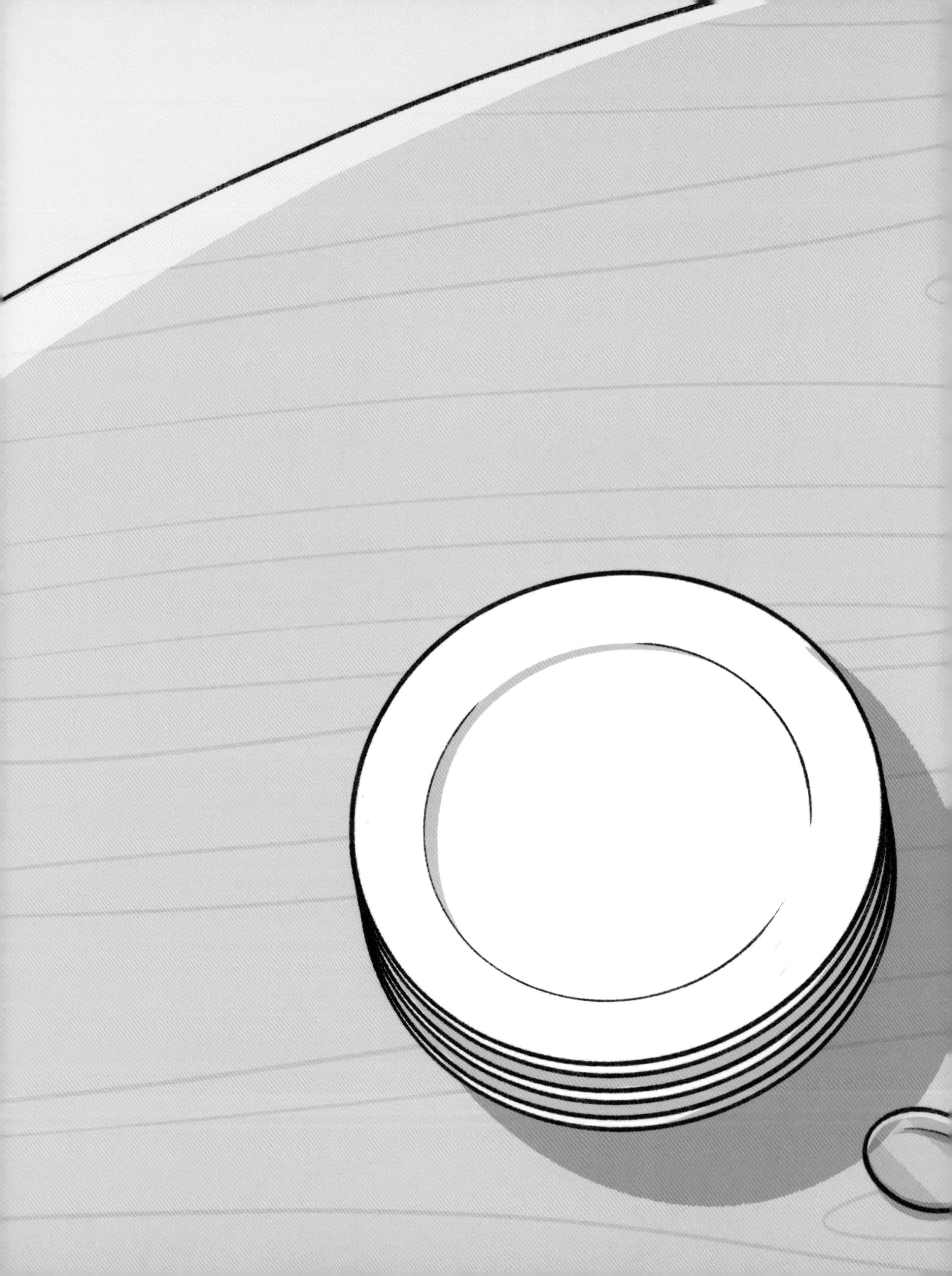

welcome home baby kingsley

About the autor

Rose Bakewell is happily married to her husband, and together, they have three beautiful children and an adorable dog named Ollie.

Rose loves British history and is an award-winning author. She is an avid baker who was chosen to be a contestant on The Great American Baking Show in England.

Her inspiration for the Lottie book series is derived from her love of baking and wanting to create a comfy cozy feeling for those who read her books.

Vanilla Extract
flour
Vinegar
Salt
Baking Soda
Vegetable Oil
Sugar
Cocoa Powder

Vanilla Extract
flour
Vinegar
Vegetable Oil
Salt
Baking Soda
Sugar
Cocoa Powder